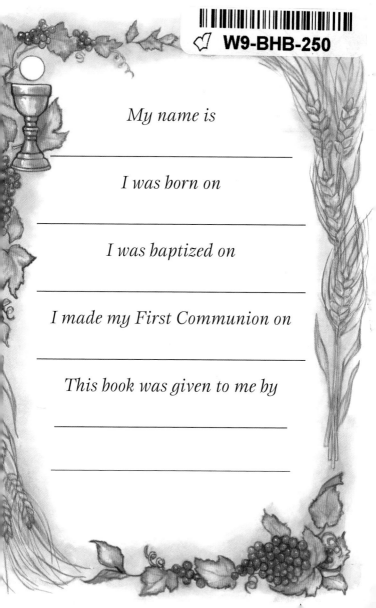

My name is

_____

I was born on

_____

I was baptized on

_____

I made my First Communion on

_____

This book was given to me by

_____

_____

Nihil Obstat:
>Rev. Brian E. Mahoney, S.T.L.

Imprimatur:
>✠Most Rev. Seán O'Malley, O.F.M. Cap.
>Archbishop of Boston
>November 10, 2004

Written by Maria Grace Dateno, FSP

Illustrated by Virginia Esquinaldo

Excerpts from the English translation of *The Roman Missal* © 2010, International Commission on English in the Liturgy Corporation. Excerpts from the English translation of *Rite of Penance* © 1974, ICEL. All rights reserved.

Published with the approval of the
Committee on Divine Worship
United States Conference of Catholic Bishops

ISBN 0-8198-4842-5

Published by Pauline Books & Media, 50 Saint Pauls Avenue, Boston, MA 02130-3491. Printed in U.S.A. www. pauline.org.

Printed in the U.S.A.

www.pauline.org

MFM VSAUSAPEOILL8-26J11-06627 4842-5

Pauline Books & Media is the publishing house of the Daughters of St. Paul, an international congregation of women religious serving the Church with the communications media.

2 3 4 5 6 7   15 14 13 12 11

Contents

It's Sunday, the Lord's Day!

Other Visits to Church

It's Sunday,

Sunday is a *special* day for us. We call it "the Lord's Day." It's a day when we go to church with other people who believe in Jesus.

Why do we go to church on Sunday? Because it's the day on which Jesus rose from the dead! The first followers or disciples of Jesus celebrated his resurrection every Sunday. They came together and did what Jesus told them to do in his memory at the Last Supper. This is what we do today at Mass, in the celebration of the Eucharist.

Lord's Day!

Sunday is special for another reason, too. It's the day on which the Holy Spirit came down on the disciples of Jesus after Jesus rose from the dead and went back to heaven. We call that day Pentecost. Pentecost was the birthday of the Church. After Pentecost, the disciples went to tell everyone the good news about Jesus.

When we go to church on Sunday, we worship God. God loves us. He made the whole world for us. We go to church to thank God. We also pray for people all over the world.

As Christians, our coming together for Mass on Sunday begins our week lived in love for God and others.

We Come Together

Introductory Rites

Entrance Song

At the beginning of Mass, we sing together. This shows how happy we are that Jesus rose from the dead! The priest, servers, and other ministers walk in procession to the front of the church. They follow the server who is carrying the cross.

Greeting

The priest says: In the name of the Father, and of the Son, and of the Holy Spirit. We answer: **Amen.**

The priest says this or another prayer like it: The grace of our Lord Jesus Christ, and the love of God, and the communion of the Holy Spirit be with you all. We answer: **And with your spirit.**

Penitential Act

Now we stop and quietly think about the wrong things we have done. We also remember the good things we *did not* do. Then, all together, we tell God we are sorry.

We say:
I confess to almighty God
and to you, my brothers and sisters,
that I have greatly sinned,
in my thoughts and in my words,
in what I have done
    and in what I have failed to do,
[We tap our chest with our right hand.]
through my fault, through my fault,
through my most grievous fault;
therefore I ask blessed Mary ever-Virgin,
all the Angels and Saints,
and you, my brothers and sisters,
to pray for me to the Lord our God.

(Sometimes we use a different prayer.)

The priest says:
May almighty God have mercy on us,
forgive us our sins,
and bring us to everlasting life.
We answer: **Amen.**

Next,

The priest says: Lord, have mercy.
We say: **Lord, have mercy.**
The priest says: Christ, have mercy.
We say: **Christ, have mercy.**
The priest says: Lord, have mercy.
We say: **Lord, have mercy.**

Gloria

Now we sing or pray together a beautiful song called the *Gloria*. We praise God the Father, Son, and Holy Spirit. We always pray the *Gloria* at Mass on Sunday, except during Advent and Lent.

We say with the priest:

Glory to God in the highest,
    and on earth peace to people of good
    will.

We praise you, we bless you,
we adore you, we glorify you,
we give you thanks for your great glory,
Lord God, heavenly King,
O God, almighty Father.

Lord Jesus Christ, Only Begotten Son,
Lord God, Lamb of God, Son of the
       Father,
you take away the sins of the world,
       have mercy on us;
you take away the sins of the world,
       receive our prayer;
you are seated at the right hand of the
       Father,
       have mercy on us.

For you alone are the Holy One,

you alone are the Lord,
you alone are the Most High,
Jesus Christ,
with the Holy Spirit,
in the glory of God the Father.
Amen.

Opening Prayer

The priest now says a prayer that is different every Sunday. We listen carefully.

At the end, we answer: **Amen.**

We Listen

Liturgy of the Word

We listen to the word of God. A reader called a *lector* reads to us from the Bible. We listen carefully because God is "speaking" to us through the reading. Then comes a special prayer from the Bible. When we sing this prayer, a singer called a cantor leads us. After this, the lector proclaims God's word again. Then the deacon or the priest proclaims a part of the Gospel and explains it to us.

First Reading

Most of the time, the first reading is from the Old Testament of the Bible. We listen to the stories of God and his chosen people, the Jews.

At the end of the reading, the reader says: The word of the Lord.
We answer: **Thanks be to God.**

Responsorial Psalm

The psalms are beautiful prayers from the Bible. We repeat the part of the psalm that the cantor or the reader sings or says at the beginning.

Second Reading

The second reading is from one of the letters written by Saint Paul or another apostle. The apostles wrote letters to the first Christians. Now these letters are part of the New Testament of the Bible.

At the end of the reading, the lector says: The word of the Lord.
We answer: **Thanks be to God.**

Alleluia or Gospel Acclamation

"Alleluia" means "praise God!" We praise and thank God for the Gospel reading that we will hear.

Gospel Reading

The Gospels are the most important part of the Bible. They tell us what Jesus said and did during his life on earth.

The priest (or deacon) says: The Lord be with you.
We answer: **And with your spirit.**

The priest (or deacon) says: A reading from the holy Gospel according to
_____ (the name of the Gospel writer).
We say: **Glory to you, O Lord.**

At the end of the Gospel reading, the priest (or deacon) says: The Gospel of the Lord.
We say: **Praise to you, Lord Jesus Christ.**

WE SIT.

14

Homily

The priest or deacon talks to us about the word of God that we have heard today. He explains how we can live as God's children by obeying all that God tells us. We listen with attention.

Profession of Faith

WE STAND.

This is a special kind of prayer called a creed. When we pray a creed we say what we believe about God and the Church. We say that we agree with what the whole Church believes and teaches.

We say together:
I believe in one God,
the Father almighty,
maker of heaven and earth,
of all things visible and invisible.

I believe in one Lord Jesus Christ,
the Only Begotten Son of God,
born of the Father before all ages.
God from God, Light from Light,
true God from true God,
begotten, not made, consubstantial with the
    Father;
through him all things were made.
For us men and for our salvation
he came down from heaven,

(Here we bow until after the words "and became man.")

and by the Holy Spirit was incarnate
of the Virgin Mary,
and became man.

For our sake he was crucified under Pontius
Pilate,
he suffered death and was buried,
and rose again on the third day
in accordance with the Scriptures.
He ascended into heaven
and is seated at the right hand of the Father.
He will come again in glory
to judge the living and the dead
and his kingdom will have no end.

I believe in the Holy Spirit, the Lord, the
giver of life,
who proceeds from the Father and the Son,
who with the Father and the Son is adored
and glorified,
who has spoken through the prophets.
I believe in one, holy, catholic and apostolic
Church.
I confess one Baptism for the forgiveness
of sins
and I look forward to the resurrection of
the dead
and the life of the world to come. Amen.

The Apostles' Creed may sometimes be used
instead.

I believe in God,
the Father almighty,

Creator of heaven and earth,
and in Jesus Christ, his only Son, our Lord,
(Here we bow until after the words "the Virgin
    Mary")
who was conceived by the Holy Spirit,
born of the Virgin Mary,
suffered under Pontius Pilate,
was crucified, died and was buried;
he descended into hell;
on the third day he rose again from the dead;
he ascended into heaven,
and is seated at the right hand of God the
    Father almighty;
from there he will come to judge the living
    and the dead.

I believe in the Holy Spirit,
the holy catholic Church,
the communion of saints,
the forgiveness of sins,
the resurrection of the body,
and life everlasting. Amen.

Prayer of the Faithful

It's time to bring to God the needs of all
people. We pray for the Church. We pray
for our country. We pray for our parish. We
pray for peace in the world and in all fami-
lies. We pray for people who have died.

After each petition, we sing or say:
"Lord, hear our prayer."

We Give Thanks

Liturgy of the Eucharist

The next part of the Mass is called the *Liturgy of the Eucharist*. The word "Eucharist" means "thanksgiving." During the Eucharistic prayer, the priest prays for all of us. He thanks God for the gifts God gives us, especially for his Son, Jesus, who gave his life for us.

WE SIT.

Presentation and Preparation of the Gifts

Now some people carry bread and wine to the priest. The bread and wine will become the Body and Blood of Jesus.

The people of the parish also give money to help the Church and the poor. The ushers collect this money and bring it to the front of the church.

The priest says these prayers before he puts the bread and wine on the altar:
Blessed are you, Lord God of all creation,
for through your goodness we have received
the bread we offer you:
fruit of the earth and work of human hands,
it will become for us the bread of life.

If the priest has said the prayer out loud, we answer: **Blessed be God for ever.**

The priest says:
Blessed are you, Lord God of all creation,
for through your goodness we have received
the wine we offer you:
fruit of the vine and work of human hands,
it will become our spiritual drink.

We answer: **Blessed be God for ever.**

Next, the priest washes his hands. Then he says:
Pray, brothers and sisters,
that my sacrifice and yours
may be acceptable to God,
the almighty Father.

WE STAND.

We answer: **May the Lord accept the sacrifice at your hands**
for the praise and glory of his name,
for our good
and the good of all his holy Church.

The priest prays a short prayer that is different every Sunday.

We answer: **Amen.**

Eucharistic Prayer

Now comes the most important part of the Mass.

The priest says: The Lord be with you.
We answer: **And with your spirit.**

The priest says: Lift up your hearts.
We answer: **We lift them up to the Lord.**

The priest says: Let us give thanks to the
Lord our God.
We answer: **It is right and just.**

Then the priest prays this prayer or another
one like it:

It is truly right and just, our duty and
    our salvation,
always and everywhere to give you
    thanks,
Lord, holy Father, almighty and eternal
    God.
For you so loved the world
that in your mercy you sent us the
    Redeemer,
to live like us in all things but sin,
so that you might love in us what you
    loved in your Son,
by whose obedience we have been
    restored to those gifts of yours
that, by sinning, we had lost in disobedi
    ence.
And so, Lord, with all the Angels and
    Saints,
we, too, give you thanks, as in exultation
    we acclaim:
(Preface VII of the Sundays in Ordinary Time)

We sing or say this prayer of praise:

Holy, Holy, Holy Lord God of hosts.

**Heaven and earth are full of your
glory.**

Hosanna in the highest.

**Blessed is he who comes in the name
of the Lord.**

Hosanna in the highest.

WE KNEEL.

We praise God for his gifts and ask the Holy
Spirit to come upon the bread and wine. We
listen carefully. The priest prays to God in our
name. He uses this prayer or one like it:

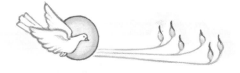

Eucharistic Prayer III

You are indeed Holy, O Lord,
and all you have created
rightly gives you praise,
for through your Son our Lord Jesus Christ,
by the power and working of the Holy Spirit,
you give life to all things and make them
holy,

and you never cease to gather a people to
	yourself,
so that from the rising of the sun to its setting
a pure sacrifice may be offered to your name.

Therefore, O Lord, we humbly implore you:
by the same Spirit graciously make holy
these gifts we have brought to you for
	consecration,
that they may become the Body and ✠ Blood
of your Son our Lord Jesus Christ,
at whose command we celebrate these
	mysteries.

**The bread and wine become the Body and
Blood of Christ.**

Priest: For on the night he was betrayed
he himself took bread,
and, giving you thanks, he said the blessing,
broke the bread and gave it to his disciples,
	saying:

> **Take this, all of you, and eat of it,
> for this is my Body,
> which will be given up for you.**

In a similar way, when supper was ended,
he took the chalice,
and, giving you thanks, he said the
	blessing,

and gave the chalice to his disciples,
  saying:

**Take this, all of you, and drink from it,
for this is the chalice of my Blood,
the Blood of the new and eternal
covenant,
which will be poured out for you
and for many
for the forgiveness of sins.
Do this in memory of me.**

The priest says or sings: The mystery of
  faith.

We say or sing: **We proclaim your Death, O
  Lord,
and profess your Resurrection
until you come again.**

  Or:
**When we eat this Bread and drink this
  Cup,
we proclaim your Death, O Lord,
until you come again.**

  Or:
**Save us, Savior of the world,
for by your Cross and Resurrection
you have set us free.**

We remember what Jesus has done for us. We
offer ourselves with him to God the Father.

Priest: Therefore, O Lord, as we celebrate
the memorial
of the saving Passion of your Son,
his wondrous Resurrection
and Ascension into heaven,
and as we look forward to his second
coming,
we offer you in thanksgiving
this holy and living sacrifice.

We pray for each other.

Priest: Look, we pray, upon the oblation of
your Church
and, recognizing the sacrificial Victim by
whose death
you willed to reconcile us to yourself,
grant that we, who are nourished
by the Body and Blood of your Son
and filled with his Holy Spirit,
may become one body, one spirit in Christ.

**We remember Mary and the saints, and we
pray that one day we will join them in heaven.**

Priest: May he make of us
an eternal offering to you,
so that we may obtain an inheritance with
    your elect,
especially with the most Blessed Virgin
    Mary, Mother of God,
with your blessed Apostles and glorious
    Martyrs
(with Saint __)
and with all the Saints,
on whose constant intercession in your
    presence
we rely for unfailing help.

We pray for the Pope and our bishop.

Priest: May this Sacrifice of our
    reconciliation,
we pray, O Lord,
advance the peace and salvation of all the
    world.
Be pleased to confirm in faith and charity
your pilgrim Church on earth,
with your servant _____ our Pope and
    _____ our Bishop,
26 the Order of Bishops, all the clergy,

and the entire people you have gained for
  your own.

**We pray for everyone in the world and for
those who have died.**

Priest: Listen graciously to the prayers of
  this family,
whom you have summoned before you:
in your compassion, O merciful Father,
gather to yourself all your children
scattered throughout the world.
To our departed brothers and sisters
and to all who were pleasing to you
at their passing from this life,
give kind admittance to your kingdom.
There we hope to enjoy for ever the fullness
  of your glory
through Christ our Lord,
through whom you bestow on the world all
  that is good.

At the end of the eucharistic prayer, the
priest holds up the host and the chalice and
says or sings:
Through him, and with him, and in him,
O God, almighty Father,
in the unity of the Holy Spirit,
all glory and honor is yours,
for ever and ever.

We say or sing together: **Amen.**

Communion Rite

WE STAND.

Now we prepare to receive Jesus in Holy Communion. We pray together the prayer Jesus taught us.

The priest says: At the Savior's command and formed by divine teaching, we dare to say:

We say: **Our Father, who art in heaven, hallowed be thy name;
thy kingdom come,
thy will be done
on earth as it is in heaven.
Give us this day our daily bread,
and forgive us our trespasses,
as we forgive those who trespass
     against us;
and lead us not into temptation,
but deliver us from evil.**

The priest says:
Deliver us, Lord, we pray, from
     every evil,
graciously grant peace in our days,
that, by the help of your mercy,
we may be always free from sin
and safe from all distress,

as we await the blessed hope
and the coming of our Savior,
    Jesus Christ.
We say: **For the kingdom,
the power and the glory are yours,
now and for ever.**

The Sign of Peace

The priest says: Lord Jesus Christ,
who said to your Apostles:
Peace I leave you, my peace I give you,
look not on our sins,
but on the faith of your Church,
and graciously grant her peace and unity
in accordance with your will.
Who live and reign for ever and ever.
We answer: **Amen.**

The priest says: The peace of the
    Lord be with you always.
We answer: **And with your spirit.**

Then the deacon or the priest says:
Let us offer each other the sign of peace.

We wish the peace of Jesus to each
other by shaking hands with the people
near us. We say, "The peace of Christ be
with you." Our sign of peace and love
shows that we want to be united to all the
members of God's Church.

Fraction (Breaking) of the Bread

Now the priest breaks the bread into smaller pieces, just as Jesus did at the Last Supper. Even though we all receive separate pieces in Holy Communion, we all receive the one Jesus. During the breaking of the bread,

We sing or say:
Lamb of God, you take away the sins
of the world, have mercy on us.
Lamb of God, you take away the sins
of the world, have mercy on us.
Lamb of God, you take away the sins
of the world, grant us peace.

WE KNEEL.

Holy Communion

The priest says: Behold the Lamb of God, behold him who takes away the sins of the world.
Blessed are those called to the supper of the Lamb.
We say with the priest:
Lord, I am not worthy
that you should enter under my roof,
but only say the word
and my soul shall be healed.

While we joyfully go up to the altar to receive Holy Communion, we may sing a song together. (To receive Communion, we need to have fasted for one hour. This means that we have not eaten or drunk anything except water for one hour before Communion.)

When I approach the priest, deacon, or extraordinary minister, I bow my head to show that I believe that Jesus is really present in the Holy Eucharist. The priest, deacon, or extraordinary minister offers me a host and says, **"The Body of Christ."**

I answer: **"Amen."** I receive the Host either on my tongue or in my hand.

At some Masses I may also receive the Blood of Christ under the appearance of wine. The priest, deacon, or extraordinary minister hands me the chalice and says, **"The Blood of Christ."**

I answer: **"Amen."** I take a sip from the chalice.

After receiving Jesus in Holy Communion, I talk to him in my heart. (Sometimes we may also sing another song together to thank Jesus for coming to us.) I can tell Jesus how much I love him. I can ask for his help for myself and for other people. I may use my own words or this prayer:

Thank you for coming into my heart, Jesus. I love you! I know that you listen to all my prayers. I can tell you everything because you are my best Friend. I want to become more like you every day. I want everyone to know and love you, too.

Here are some special things I want to pray for . . . (tell Jesus whatever is in your heart).

Please take care of my parents and family, Jesus. Please help all those who are sick or suffering in any way. Please let everyone in the world live in love and peace. Thank you for everything, Jesus. Amen.

WE STAND.

Prayer after Communion

After everyone has received Communion, the priest says a prayer that changes every Sunday.

We answer: **Amen.**

We Go in Love

Concluding Rite

We get ready to go home now. Our hearts are filled with the love of Jesus. We are happy to go and bring that love to everyone we meet this week.

The priest says: The Lord be with you.
We answer: **And with your spirit.**

Blessing

The priest blesses us with these words:
May almighty God bless you,
the Father, and the Son, ✠ and the
    Holy Spirit.
We make the sign of the cross and
answer: **Amen.**

Dismissal

Now the deacon (or priest), says or sings: Go forth, the Mass is ended.
We answer: **Thanks be to God.**

We sing a song to end our celebration of the Mass.

Other Visits

Besides going to church on Sundays for the celebration of Mass, it is very good to go at other times, too. We may stop in to make a visit to Jesus in the Holy Eucharist. We may come to church to pray morning and evening prayer with other members of our parish.

Church

We may come to pray the Rosary or the Stations of the Cross together. We also come to church to celebrate the sacrament of Penance or Reconciliation.

Visit to the Blessed Sacrament

We can pray anywhere because prayer is talking to God, and God is everywhere! But Jesus is present in a very special way in our churches. He is present in all the Hosts that are consecrated at Mass. We call these consecrated Hosts the *Holy Eucharist* or the *Blessed Sacrament*. Some of these consecrated Hosts are always kept in the *tabernacle*. (A tabernacle is a beautiful box-like shrine.) That way, Holy Communion can be brought to sick people who can't come to Mass. A candle is kept burning near the tabernacle to remind us that Jesus is there.

Jesus is also present in the Blessed Sacrament for us to adore and worship him. Sometimes, a large consecrated Host may be placed in a stand called a *monstrance*. The monstrance lets us see the Blessed Sacrament while we pray. This is called *Eucharistic exposition*.

Here is a prayer to Jesus in the Blessed Sacrament:

Jesus, I am happy to be able to come visit you.
You loved us so much that you gave us the gift of the Eucharist.
Thank you for coming to me in Holy Communion.
Thank you for always being here in the Blessed Sacrament, ready to listen to me.
These are the special things I want to pray for . . . (tell Jesus about all the people and situations you want to pray for).

I am sorry for the times I have not behaved as you would want me to.
Help me to follow you more closely.
Thank you for being my friend, Jesus.
I love you. Amen.

Here is another prayer you can use when you make a visit to Jesus in the Blessed Sacrament:

Jesus, I believe that you are really here in the Blessed Sacrament.

I am sorry for the times I have offended you. I promise that from now on I will try to be good, obedient, and kind.

Help me to grow in love for you and for everyone, Jesus. Amen.

Sacrament of Reconciliation

The sacrament of Penance or Reconciliation is a great gift from Jesus. Through this sacrament, we experience God's forgiveness in a wonderful way.

Everyone in the Church is called to follow Jesus and to live the way he taught us. But we don't always do this. Sometimes we make mistakes. Sometimes we don't obey the Ten Commandments and we sin. When we hurt others or ourselves, or fail to treat them with respect, we sin.

We receive God's forgiveness in the sacrament of Reconciliaton. But we also receive something else that is very special—God's grace. Grace is the help that we need to live as God wants us to.

There are six steps to follow in celebrating the sacrament of Reconciliation:

1. *Think* of your sins.

2. *Be sorry* for them.

3. *Confess* (tell) your sins to the priest.

4. *Promise* Jesus that you will try not to sin again.

5. *Receive* God's forgiveness through absolution, which the priest says.

6. *Do or pray* the *penance* the priest gives you.

Celebrating the sacrament of Reconciliation helps us to live as the family of God!

My Examination of Conscience

We get ready to receive the sacrament of Reconciliation by remembering how much God loves us. Then we think about the times we have not followed Jesus and have not obeyed the Ten Commandments. This is called the *examination of conscience*.

You can say this prayer before you make your examination of conscience:

Lord, help me to remember the times that I have offended you and other people. Help me to be sorry. Fill me with love!

Here are the *Ten Commandments* and some questions that will help you to make your examination of conscience:

1. I am the Lord your God: you shall not have strange gods before me.

Did I make anything more important to me than God? Did I say my prayers every day?

2. You shall not take the name of the Lord, your God, in vain.

Did I use the name of God or of Jesus disrespectfully?

3. Remember to keep holy the Lord's Day.

Did I go to Mass every Sunday (or Saturday evening) and try hard to pay attention?

4. Honor your father and your mother.

Did I respect and obey my parents and those who have authority over me?

5. You shall not kill.

Was I kind and helpful to my brothers and sisters, friends and neighbors (even those I don't like very much)? Did I hurt anyone by my words or actions? Did I make fun of others or leave them out of games? Have I avoided drugs and anything else that would harm me?

6. You shall not commit adultery.

Have I treated my body and everyone else's body with respect? Is my language clean? Have I watched only good TV shows and movies? Have I read only good books and magazines and looked at only good things on the internet?

7. You shall not steal.

Have I stolen anything? Have I always returned things I borrowed? Did I cheat in schoolwork?

8. You shall not bear false witness.

Have I lied about others? Do I always tell the truth, even when it's hard?

9. You shall not covet your neighbor's wife.

Have I been jealous of the friends of others?

10. You shall not covet your neighbor's goods.

Do I wish I had what belongs to someone else? Am I grateful for all I have, including the talents God has given me?

My Confession

When you are ready, go into the reconciliation room or the confessional. After you sit or kneel down, the priest will greet you.

The priest says: In the name of the Father, and of the Son, and of the Holy Spirit.

You make the Sign of the Cross and answer: **Amen.**

(Sometimes the priest may also read a short reading from the Bible.)

Now you tell your sins to the priest. You should also tell him how long it has been since your last confession.

The priest will listen to you. He may also give you some advice to help you to try to do better from now on.

Then the priest will give you a penance. This could be prayers to say or good deeds to do.

Next the priest will invite you to say an act of contrition (a prayer of sorrow for your sins). You can pray this one or any one you know:

My God,
I am sorry for my sins with all my
    heart.
In choosing to do wrong and failing to
    do good,
I have sinned against you
whom I should love above all things.
I firmly intend, with your help,
to do penance,
to sin no more,
and to avoid whatever leads me to sin.

Our Savior Jesus Christ
suffered and died for us.
In his name, my God,
    have mercy.

The priest then holds his hands over your
head and says these words of forgiveness
in the name of God:

God, the Father of mercies,
through the death and resurrection of his
    Son
has reconciled the world to himself
and sent the Holy Spirit among us
for the forgiveness of sins;
through the ministry of the Church
may God give you pardon and peace,
and I absolve you from your sins
in the name of the Father, and of the Son,
and of the Holy Spirit.
You answer: **Amen**.

Then the priest says: Give thanks to the
    Lord for he is good.
You answer: **His mercy endures for ever.**

The priest tells you to go in peace.

After Confession

Do your penance as soon as possible, so that you don't forget it. The penance we are given helps us to make up for what we have done wrong. It also helps us to change our life and become more like Jesus.

You can also say this prayer to thank Jesus:

Thank you, Jesus, for the gift of this sacrament. I am so happy to know that you have forgiven me! Help me to try harder to love you as you love me. Help me to love others as you want me to. Amen.

BOOKS & MEDIA

The Daughters of St. Paul operate book and media centers at the following addresses. Visit, call or write the one nearest you today, or find us on the World Wide Web, www.pauline.org

CALIFORNIA

3908 Sepulveda Blvd, Culver City,
CA 90230 310-397-8676

935 Brewster Avenue, Redwood
City, CA 94063 650-369-4230

5945 Balboa Avenue, San Diego,
CA 92111 858-565-9181

FLORIDA

145 S.W. 107th Avenue, Miami,
FL 33174 305-559-6715

HAWAII

1143 Bishop Street, Honolulu,
HI 96813 808-521-2731

Neighbor Islands call:
866-521-2731

ILLINOIS

172 North Michigan Avenue,
Chicago, IL 60601
312-346-4228

LOUISIANA

4403 Veterans Memorial Blvd,
Metairie, LA 70006
504-887-7631

MASSACHUSETTS

885 Providence Hwy, Dedham,
MA 02026 781-326-5385

MISSOURI

9804 Watson Road, St. Louis,
MO 63126 314-965-3512

NEW YORK

64 West 38th Street, New York,
NY 10018 212-754-1110

PENNSYLVANIA

Relocating 215-676-9494

SOUTH CAROLINA

243 King Street, Charleston,
SC 29401 843-577-0175

VIRGINIA

1025 King Street, Alexandria,
VA 22314 703-549-3806

CANADA

3022 Dufferin Street, Toronto,
ON M6B 3T5 416-781-9131

¡También somos su fuente para libros, videos y música en español!